S0-APM-207

I'm sorry
I tagged
that picture
of you on
Facebook.

I'm
sorry
I came
in your
eye.

sorry

I'm sorry you got caught with my stash.

sorry

I'm
sorry
I
ruined
your
birthday.

I'm sorry
I hit you
in the
penis.

I'm sorry I clogged your toilet.

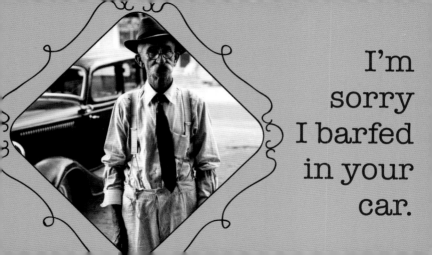

I'm
sorry
I barfed
in your
car.

I'm sorry your parents think I'm a slut.

I'm sorry
I called
you my
ex's name.

I'm
sorry I
walked
in on
you.

I'm sorry
I tried to
spice things
up without
asking first.

I'm
sorry
I puked
on you.

I'm sorry
I hit on
your
girlfriend
right in
front of you.

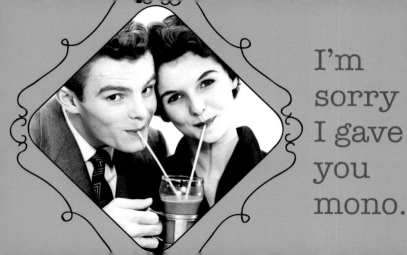

I'm
sorry
I gave
you
mono.

I'm sorry
I make
so many
poor
choices.

sorry

I'm sorry
I stopped
following
you on
Twitter.

I'm
sorry
I ruined
the
clothes
you let me
borrow.

I'm sorry I got us 86'd from the bar.

sorry

I'm sorry I smoked all of your pot.

sorry

I'm sorry I had sex on your bed.